RIVERS OF GREEN WISDOM

To Terry
and Sheila
Best wishes.

from
Santoshan
(Stephen Wollaston)

GreenSpirit book series

RIVERS of GREEN WISDOM

Exploring Christian and Yogic Earth Centred Spirituality

**Santoshan
(Stephen Wollaston)**

Published by GreenSpirit
137 Ham Park Road, London E7 9LE
www.greenspirit.org.uk

Registered Charity No. 1045532

ISBN: 9798783667695 (hardback) / 978-0-9935983-2-6 (paperback)

Design and artwork by Santoshan (Stephen Wollaston)
Printed by CreateSpace and Amazon

Front cover image © Binkski/Shutterstock.com
Page 45 photos © Santoshan (Stephen Wollaston)

Contents

To all who have sought a more caring and
compassionate Earth-life.

A special thanks to
Marian Van Eyk McCain for assisting with the proof
reading, and to Ian Mowll for helping to clarify some
matters of Christian belief. But it goes without saying that
any errors that might remain are entirely my own.

Publisher's Preface

This is the first of two especially linked titles in the GreenSpirit Book Series. For this title the author, at our request, has drawn on specific passages from two of his key works that touched on Yogic, Christian and Nature centred spiritualities, *The House of Wisdom* (co-authored) and *Spirituality Unveiled*, and added further reflections and personal experiences encountered while exploring these enriching traditions. The second title, *Pathways of Green Wisdom*, which has been edited and compiled by Santoshan/Stephen, brings together numerous reflective, insightful and informative pieces by various contributors to our magazine spanning a period of 11 years, along with especially written new material.

The GreenSpirit Book Series is a low-cost series sold at production price only. *Rivers of Green Wisdom* is the fourth title in this collection. Other titles planned will look at the application of green spiritual principles to different aspects of life and culture such as ecology, education, personal spiritual practice, and ritual.

GreenSpirit is a registered charity based in the UK.

The main contents/written material, editing, design and promotional work for our books is done on a purely voluntary basis, or given freely by contributors who share our passion for Gaia centred spirituality.

* * *

Introduction

If we learn to love the earth, we will find labyrinths,
gardens, fountains, and precious jewels!
A whole new world will open itself to us.
We will discover what it means to be truly alive.
— Teresa of Avila.

In *A Tale of Two Cities* by Charles Dickens, the opening line mentions how, "It was the best of times, it was the worst of times, it was the age of wisdom, it was the age of foolishness". Although written some 150 years ago, these words seem to ring just as true for our current era. With the touch of a button we have the world's past and present scientific knowledge and spiritual insights at our finger tips. Never before has there been a time when we have been so informed about global issues and ways in which we are linked to the creativity of the universe and all life on Earth. Yet with all this knowledge there is a lack of wisdom regarding the welfare of Earth. Damage is being done by us humans on a grand scale that it is affecting Nature's biodiversity and ecological balance.

Yet there is hope, and there are influential voices of

our age that are having and have had an impact on current thinking and how to move healthily forward. Many of those mentioned in this book have achieved more unitive paths and encouraged a more responsible spirituality relevant for our times and is why I have included them. Although people especially picked-out in this book are mainly from Christian and Yogic traditions, there are in fact prophets to be found in all disciplines and spiritual paths. The first draft of the Earth Charter for instance, a declaration of fundamental principles for building a just, sustainable and peaceful world, was compiled by people from various backgrounds in 1997. Germany has recently made great inroads in replacing fossil burning fuels for energy to more environmentally friendly alternatives. In Madagascar the government and local groups have started to show transient farmers how to grow crops in productive but environmentally safe ways in areas where overcrowding had caused serious deforestation.

Collectively, the essential call of contemporary prophets is for a just and sustainable Earth community, for us to reassess our values and actions and discover simpler and more responsible living that treads lightly upon our beautiful planet. In place of violent acts against Nature and trying to prove that any one tradition is superior to another, as the Anglo-Saxon missionary Boniface did when he cut down the sacred oak of the Germanic pagans, there is a need for us to accept our differences and work together for a greater good.

The seas are gradually turning for an environmentally

conscious age, not only on the edges of religious traditions, but also within the depths of them. Pope John Paul II called for a new ecological awareness in 1990. Pope Francis deliberately chose the name of the patron saint of animals, and has become a major advocate of enviromental protection and important green issues. Some American evangelical Christians have even become ecological converts. Many progressive green conscious Christians have also revived and reintegrated Celtic and other Earth centred traditions within their daily lives. Within such changes there is joy to be found in the wisdom and practices people are discovering and embracing. Traditional artistic routes involve dancing, singing, painting, sculpting, writing, drumming and storytelling, as found and practised in various cultures. Whether we are artists, shamans, carpenters, students, nurses, teachers, labourers, yogis, activists, priests or healers, there are numerous profound ways of making our daily actions a dedication to skilful, wholesome, compassionate, fair and just living that encompasses the protection and welfare of all that exists on, with, and as an amazing part of Earth. "[E]ach tree is known by its own fruit", Jesus reminds us in Luke's Gospel (6:44).

In chapter 10 of the Bhagavad Gita, Krishna teaches Prince Arjuna about his all-pervasive nature permeating the flowing rivers of the Ganges, the beginning and end of creation, the wind, the fish and the banyan tree. The great rishis of the ancient Upanishads saw *Brahman*/divinity in all. The Rig Veda, which contains the oldest hymns of the Hindu tradition, highlights a belief in a natural order operating within the universe, termed *rita* in Sanskrit, which early brahmin priests sought to help maintain and be in communion with through rituals and prayers. Also connected with India's spiritual past were the people of the ancient Indus Valley Civilisation, who discovered creative ways of farming and irrigation that were in balance with Nature. Now more than ever we need to recognise, preserve, cherish and respect the sacredness of life surrounding us and once again understand and live in harmony with Gaia's ways, take joy in her beauty and the diversity of life and species she has sought to celebrate.

When we awaken to these nourishing fields of awareness, we come to realise the same spiritual insights as the prophets and mystics of both the past and present, such as the late Thomas Berry (who preferred to call himself a *geologian* rather than a *theologian*) who profoundly recognised that, "To wantonly destroy another species is to silence a divine voice forever".

*   *   *

1
Pursuing Meaning and Purpose

My parents had only partial interests in religious or spiritual matters and only attended church if there was a wedding, funeral or christening. At junior school, there was just one person my age I knew who went to a close-by Anglican church. On the couple of occasions I ventured along with him to check it out, I found myself feeling out of place, lectured to, and confused about what I was meant to do and why, such as when to stand up or sit down on a cold and hard wooden pew.

As young as I was back then (around nine to ten years old), I had started to contemplate existential ideas about dying and eternal existence and had had one or two unusual experiences relating to non-physical dimensions of awareness. I had two bad road accidents at the ages of seven and eleven. Immediately after the first one occurred, I was placed in a hospital bed next to a boy who died from severe head injuries sustained from a simple fall. It therefore comes as no surprise that I had started to reflect upon matters of life and death at an early age. But as I witnessed the service at my local church, I wondered how any of it was relevant to my life. There was nothing that resonated with me, any of my experiences or thoughts about existence. I was also aware of a certain amount of class suspicion within the church congregation (kids are often more intuitively aware of situations than adults realise). My family was working class and we lived in only one of two East London council houses in an area of otherwise privately owned properties. So you can imagine, the majority of people attending our nearest church were on the whole from more prestigious backgrounds than my London Transport bus driver father and factory worker, clothes presser mother.

School life wasn't much better for learning anything beneficial about religious beliefs or spiritual teachings and experience and how they could be applied creatively to life in any helpful way. When I was a pupil in the 60s, the only time my RE class ever became interesting was when my secondary school teacher Mr Phelps took whatever opportunity he could to go off-topic and talk about his main passion, which was jazz, or to reminisce about his years as a soldier in World War II. As stimulating as this sometimes was, I learned little about Christianity, other world religions, mysticism or spirituality. Hardly surprising, I gave Christian and other religious and spiritual teachings little thought for some time after these early encounters.

Enrichment in Creativity and Nature

As well as playing in a rock band with older musicians during my school years (one of them was a drummer and friend called Johnny Rich who I also played with in the 70s punk band The Wasps, and still remain friends with today), I pencil-sketched reams of pictures whenever I could and quite naturally discovered 'art as meditation', enjoyed quiet moments in my parents' garden, ran energetically around with friends and my family's dog in local grassland parks and nearby exquisite densely wooded regions of Epping Forest, and enjoyed family outings to the sea or countryside. I possess fond memories of enjoyable excursions and times of pretend play, such as being a member of Robin Hood's gang of philanthropic rebels. Though my junior school reports highlighted the same old complaint time and time again about being 'a dreamer', as though imagination had no valuable role in life or education, especially a child's life and education! Luckily, my parents didn't see anything wrong with being imaginative. After all, it wasn't as if there were no problems with the almost Dickensian education system that might explain why I sometimes preferred to let my mind take off someplace else. If only I'd known Albert Einstein's views, who famously said, "Imagination is more valuable than knowledge". For it is imagination that supplies us with the ability to put ourselves in other species and people's shoes and empathise with their struggles, needs and suffering, and through this unfold spontaneous acts of compassion along with other creative and valuable spiritual gifts.

I would lose myself for hours drawing, being in amazing and magical green spaces, creating and playing music, or simply staring wondrously at the shapes of mesmerising morphing clouds and the gyrating activity of bees hopping from flower to flower while they made intriguing buzzsaw-like sounds. At this point, I hadn't discovered how different facets of life, creativity, Nature and experience could come together and be seen as integral facets of important Earth centred spiritualities that radically addressed the needs of our current age. 'Spirituality' to me in my early years meant 'religion'. And 'religion' meant beliefs and finger wagging moralities propagated to force people such as myself to behave in a way conservative middle-class society and the Church considered appropriate. This generally implied, as far as I could grasp back then, keeping me in my place and hardly having any enjoyment at all! Yet this understanding was all to change quite dramatically...

Strange Gurus and Radical Mystics

The 60s and the 70s became a memorable time for Western seekers exploring a plethora of Eastern traditions, teachings and practices. Along with others, The Beatles famously flew to India to learn transcendental meditation under the guidance of Maharishi Mahesh Yogi, and various Indian gurus' teachings, such as Swami Muktananda and Swami Prabhupada's, spread in the West to promote numerous beneficial aspects of Yoga philosophy and practice. Members of Prabhupada's Hare Krishna movement, ISKCON (International Society for Krishna Consciousness), were to be found at various rock and folk festivals. For some years now they have run a successful cow protection programme at Bhaktivedanta Manor in England and have helped develop farming communities around the world. When I came across the movement in the early 70s they had more of an aggressive proselytising style for spreading their message that I personally found off-putting, though I did like that they were vegetarians, which I also became for spiritual and ethical reasons. Because of a recent mild health problem, I was able to follow a vegetarian diet more thoroughly those days.

I ought to mention at this point that the Sanskrit word 'Yoga' comes from the verbal root *yuj*, meaning 'to yoke/bind together' and is often interpreted as unity with the divine. Many schools of Yoga include the famous eight limbs of Patanjali's Yoga Sutra (often termed 'Classical' or 'Raga/Royal' Yoga), which, like other teachings of Yoga, encourages the cultivation of positive qualities, including taking joy in other's successes, equanimity and unfolding compassion, friendliness and a non-harmful temperament. These are in fact identical to Buddhism's four sublime states. Yet Yoga itself is not a religion, but refers to different spiritual practices and paths that are essential elements of various Indian traditions, such as Buddhism, Hinduism and Jainism. The word 'Hinduism' it should also be mentioned is merely an umbrella term that has come into use to define various beliefs that have numerous interwoven links with different devotional, philosophical and spiritual traditions, practices and the ancient Vedas and Upanishads. The West could be said to have its own unique forms of Yoga, such as transpersonal psychology and eco-psychology, contemplative prayer and Neo-Paganism. But nothing develops in isolation and within these there can be found direct connections to or traces of Eastern influences.

For many, the initial 60s explosion of interest in different traditions had a huge impact. But when that first burst of activity appeared, I was only a young school kid. It was to be a few years later, when I met and played with an older guitarist, Sid Worth, who was known in my area for running a popular music venue in the East End of London that things quickly changed. Sid, it turned out, knew some sound basics of Yogic mystical teachings and meditation, and was only too keen to help me grasp what they were about. It wasn't long before I personally encountered various experiences of what some of those *strange gurus*, as they initially appeared to me back then, were teaching. The insights and practices Sid shared, though simple, were, for me, profound. They touched me deeply and mysteriously opened my mind to other levels of life, not only inwardly, but also outwardly. In an odd way, it was as though I already knew the truth of the teachings, but had somehow never been aware that I knew them before. Yogic wisdom about a non-separate interconnected oneness (often termed 'non-dualism' or 'unitive consciousness' in mystical traditions) and how every person, thing, creature, rock, plant, tree and stream are creative expressions of an underlying divinity just blew me away.

I later discovered that these insights were not solely the teachings of Indian yogis. They were in fact crucial to a vast majority of mystics from numerous traditions, including Christianity, which up to that point no one had bothered to tell me about and seemed to have been keeping secret for some peculiar reason. For mystics, the same as artists, can be people who are sometimes feared, as they can shake things up, step outside of the accepted norms and dare to question things from wider perspectives that others may find difficult to achieve. It's the reason why they are not always popular, as they can rock the boat, undermine the status quo and teachings that are no longer pertinent for the time. Rather than face reality, those who are not ready to accept what needs bringing into awareness often then start projecting all kinds of negative baggage onto others, especially onto those seeking for or introducing a new vision or highlighting what is being overlooked.

Within GreenSpirit's aims, the prophetic voices of poets, artists and mystics are cherished and is one of the key reasons why I have remained an active member, as GreenSpirit is one of only a few spiritual groups I know that embraces, encourages and understands the creative process, artists and deeper mysteries of creativity. Sadly, there have been times when I have had to stand back from some organisations when there's been a lack of this type of progressive thinking and inclusiveness.

GreenSpirit has been very much influenced by the four elements/routes of the creation mystical journey (1. *via positivia*, 2. *via negativa*, 3. *via creativa,* and 4. *via transformativa*) that the Episcopal priest, radical theologian and activist Matthew Fox has done much to revive and bring to our attention in recent decades. The 3rd element is a call to be co-creators with God, which can be achieved through art as meditation, where we trust our creative thoughts and give birth to and take responsibility for them – as creativity can also be destructive as well as beneficial to life, humanity, society and Earth. It is about being known through what we do, and knowing our hidden treasures, gifts and abilities and skilfully manifesting them. Green/creation centred spirituality embraces an understanding of the divine as continuously creating and being present within all things. This contrasts sharply with rigid fundamentalist ideas of creation that promote a *literal* belief in a series of events happening within a relatively not too distant past, starting creation and completing it within six days.

*   *   *

2
Opening to Greater Awareness

When I looked more deeply into the mystical traditions of India and Christianity, I discovered that they can have different teachings and philosophies about the physical world, about existence and the creation of the universe. Augustine of Hippo (354-430 CE), who developed the concept of original sin, and some schools of Advaita Vedanta philosophy, viewed physical life as tainted, as something to be denied rather than affirmed, cherished and celebrated. Yet some, such as the medieval Rhineland mystic Hildegard of Bingen, and the great 11th century Hindu philosopher and sage Ramanuja, were more holistic, life affirming and creation centred. For Ramanuja, Earth was seen as Vishnu's/God's body. Similarly, Origen of Alexandria (185-254 CE) likened the entire world to the body of Christ. John Chryssavgis, a clergyman of the Greek Orthodox Archdiocese of America, pointed out that "the Eastern Christian Church defined the relationship between God and creation by affirming that creation was charged with divine energy, that nothing was outside the embrace of God".

It should be mentioned that Augustine's non-biblical concept of original sin, in which humankind is seen as born inherently guilty of the rebellion committed by Adam in the Garden of Eden, never became a teaching of the Eastern Orthodox Church or for the majority of Jewish believers. Before the 2nd century Bishop of Lyon, Irenaeus, who was the first to allude to the concept, there was no mention of it in the early Jesus movements (the plural is deliberate here as it is now believed there were various early Christian movements with different teachings and practices). Instead, one's original nature was often seen as pure, and life and creation were viewed as divine gifts from God – an idea that was central to influential Christian Nature mystics such as Hildegard and Francis of Assisi, and can be found in Paul's letter to the Romans, where he declares that God's invisible qualities, eternal power and divine nature can be clearly seen in the things that have been made (1:20). This cosmic and Nature based understanding of spirituality is also found in sacred Hindu images of dancing Shiva (Shiva-Nataraj), where he is depicted dancing in the heart of all creation.

Nonetheless, it was my first encounter (mentioned in the previous chapter) with Yogic wisdom that triggered the big 'wow!' factor for me and started a snowball rolling that got broader and broader the more it gained momentum. It also helped me through a difficult period when I reached the age of 19 and found myself battling with troubling feelings, inner conflicts and suicidal thoughts. This led to what many Western psychologists like calling 'a peak experience' (a term used by the American psychologist Abraham Maslow to describe transcendent experiences of interconnectedness, wholeness, euphoria, awe and wonder). The term itself I'm slightly gun wary of, as it's *sometimes* used differently to how Maslow intended in an attempt to shoot-down and dismiss spiritual or mystical implications of numerous life-transforming experiences, in place of valuing their positive effects and deeper implications. Looking back, I believe the experience happened because new doors were opening and awakening my awareness to identifying previously unhelpful and inhibiting ways of being. An old skin was in need of shedding. An unlearning stage was required.

Things happened unexpectedly one summer's afternoon when I was alone at my parents' home and suddenly felt impelled to be quiet and still and sat in an old armchair in the backroom of the house. In spite of my state of mind, the day was bright and sunny. The shaded room overlooked the garden. I could hear the outdoor wild birds singing and the sound of a square orange plastic wall clock rhythmically ticking away in the room. The experience that immediately unfolded involved an amazing release of troubling feelings and restrictive thoughts and helped me to see things with fresh eyes. I became conscious of a sacred presence, of which the ticking of the clock, the singing of the birds outside, the silence of the house, what felt like another mind widening, communing and blending with mine, and a clear awareness of both my physical body and being more than it, all became intertwined facets of one another. It was that mind blowing interconnected oneness again, but on a much grander scale than I had experienced before, which from that day on, became an influential episode that has never left me.

Although it was a major turning point, I can't say it instantly changed my whole life. It did, however, plant seeds that later flourished and led me in directions I could never have imaged. In spite of leaving school at 15 with no academic skills or qualifications, I found myself taking a deep interest in numerous mystical and Nature centred traditions and went on to study world religions, philosophy, education and aspects of psychology at King's College, University of London. A female swami and a former Christian monk, also approached me to write books with them. My previous hedonistic rock musician lifestyle also organically changed as I became more healthily in touch with more authentic levels of being.

Authentic Yoga

In the Yogic traditions, a true guru is one that helps her or his students find the ultimate guru, which is seen as both the divine and the teacher within oneself, all things and life. Within authentic strands of Yoga there are three principal paths mentioned: Bhakti (path of devotion), Karma (path of actions) and Jnana (path of wiseful, intuitive and mystical knowledge). Yet it would be hard for these to be practised in total isolation from one another. For example, Bhakti, in its truest sense, connects with both the body and the mind. For it requires intuitive knowledge and understanding one's true Self and its implications (the path of Jnana Yoga), which naturally leads to the practice of unconditionally giving one's self and altruistic actions in the world (the path of Karma Yoga practised in an ethical way). From this it can be seen how the three principal pathways of Yoga easily overlap when practised at their highest.

Within Hindu and Yoga philosophy and psychology there is mention of seven main chakras/energy points, of which the base/root chakra, *muladhara*, is especially looked upon as connected to the physical body and to Earth from which the body draws its vitality and energy. There is also mention of the three *gunas*/qualities (*sattva*/purity; *ragas*/energy and material desires; and *tamas*/inertia and dullness) that are seen to interact continuously with each other and affect our actions. Various types of food and places, such as mountains and cities, are said to possess different vibrations of the *gunas*. At the most basic level of psychological and ethical understanding, the *gunas* can be looked upon in the following ways:

1. Sattvic Actions

Actions that create harmony, are responsible, balanced, mindful and pure, flow spontaneously and freely from our nature, and connect with and consider others and the environment.

2. Rajasic Actions

Actions that are influenced by self-centred desires, which cause a strain on our relationships with others and the environment, and arise from a belief in self-importance.

3. Tamasic Actions

Actions that are performed from a confused, unclear and unthought-through state of mind, which are irresponsible, have little consideration for the outcome, cause offence and harm other people and life.

From a spiritual standpoint we see how the more negative actions summarised above would need transforming and how the cultivation of *sattvic* actions is more spiritually beneficial. Yet there are other teachings that mention *rajasic* activity playing a key role in the creation of the universe and in the hustle and bustle of daytime activity, and *tamas* influencing us when we rest in the evenings and at night. The following is a further example given in James Fadiman and Robert Frager's excellent *Personality and Personal Growth*: "In the process of creating a statue, for example, tamas can be seen in the untouched, inert stone. Ragas is the act of carving, and sattva is the image in the sculptor's imagination." Overall, the psychological ideal is about expanding our consciousness, being aware of and purifying, balancing and spiritualising different facets of ourselves and becoming more in harmony with life.

Christian Spirituality

My interest and more beneficial contact (compared with my early experiences) with Christian spirituality emerged in a roundabout way. As I began to read widely about the insights of various influential Indian teachers, such as Paramahansa Yogananda and Swami Vivekananda, who helped to bring Yogic wisdom to the West in the 19th and 20th centuries, I quickly picked-up on them seeking to encourage healthy dialogues with other traditions and including important teachings of Jesus in their works.

Although biblical scholars recognise John's Gospel to be very different to the other three canonical Gospels and see it as seeking to associate Jesus with the divine logos and emphasising his *unique* status, Yogananda understood it in a slightly different way. He wrote at great length about the Cosmic Christ Consciousness and looked for more universal interpretations of the Christian idea of coming to God through Jesus (John 14:6). Like other contemporary progressive writers and teachers on Christianity, Yogananda understood the passage in John as referring to a way of realising mystical oneness with the divine, which links with Jesus's own saying of being one with God (John 10:30). A religious studies teacher I once knew understood John 14:6 as being about a way to God *for Christians* and believed that for people of other faiths, there were different paths that could be taken.

Perceptions such as Yogananda's release passages in John from exclusive interpretations and turn Jesus's insights into an all-embracing, inclusive message of mystical unity that falls outside the boundaries of controlling church dogma. Importantly, such insights link with numerous authentic mystical paths that remind us we are born with the same capacity to discover awe, wonder, divine mystery and non-dual unity with the sacredness of all life within and around us – what Christian writers and teachers such as the Episcopal priest and modern-day mystic Cynthia Bourgeault refer to as the 'divine indwelling'.

Such inclusiveness, along with contact with new Christian friends who lived their faith in wholesome ways, as well as much needed silent contemplative retreats at monasteries in the UK, helped me reassess the tradition I had dismissed in childhood with new understanding. It also led me to the wiseful Earth centred works of Matthew Fox and Thomas Berry, Christian scholars such as Elaine Pagels and Marcus Borg on early Jesus movements, and Cynthia Bourgeault and Thomas Keating on centring prayer, mysticism and the wisdom of Jesus.

These pioneering and influential figures have looked deeply at spirituality in open, inclusive and radical ways that are both practical and beneficial for the times in which we live. Obviously Fox and Berry are especially pertinent to the underlying focus of this book, for they have particularly understood human creativity as being a part of the creativity of Nature and the universe and how we interconnect with and share collective responsibilities for the natural world. Nonetheless, for someone like myself, who has also taken an interest in contemporary findings about the roots of Christian wisdom, I feel Pagels and

Borg's writings are indispensable, as are Bourgeault and Keating's enlightening talks and books on centring prayer. For there is often a need for understanding our past, our country's own spiritual traditions, along with other pathways. This is not about reading or gaining information for intellectual knowledge, but for deepening our spirituality, which leads to an authentic awakening to the sacredness of all life. This often involves (as I discovered in the experience I mentioned earlier in this chapter) unlearning things that previously restricted our vision.

Just as we find a sense of the sacred in the awe we experience when seeing beauty in a setting sun, there is as much sacred and deep beauty in spiritual insights and teachings of both the past and the present that remind us profoundly of our true relationships with all, which help us find divinity and nourishment in everyday activities and support us in facing contemporary issues with wisdom.

Outside the Box

Before I became aware of various wise Christian masters, I became and remained best friends with the renowned contemporary teacher, medium and former Benedictine monk Glyn Edwards (who was also known by his given Yoga name Devadasa, meaning 'servant of God'), who found being amongst Nature an essential part of his spiritual life. Interestingly, students on his courses came from a variety of traditions and from teenage years to senior citizens. He was the first person I came across to have read so widely and to have taken a keen interest in an array of essential areas, such as scientific discoveries, world religions, mysticism, environmental issues and psychology. He also kept a strong interest in the lives and teachings of various Christian mystics and Christian spirituality. His influence helped me to be aware of key contemporaries such as the French palaeontologist, priest and mystic Teilhard de Chardin, and the English Benedictine monk Bede Griffiths. While discovering such towering giants of spirituality, I realised that the reason why their work is still so well remembered today is that so few people have radically thought outside of the box and explored the spiritualities needed for their time in the way those two had done.

Around this period (late 1980s) I also began to investigate benefits of spiritual retreats at different centres. One small community had 80 acres of wild forest surrounding it. It was there while on a regular morning walk under a cathedral-like ceiling of tree branches stretching over a mottled light-grey and brown stony forest path that I realised I was finding a deeper serenity and spirituality amongst Mother Nature than in many communities' chapels. This wasn't to say that *creative* rituals that looked for deeper ways to touch life profoundly didn't have value. But somehow the natural world was calling me to another mystery that was often absent from even the most moving of church and temple services, which went beyond words, set rituals and prayers. This in many ways reminds me of a quotation I recently read by Ikkyu in Llewellyn Vaughan-Lee's *Spiritual Ecology*: "Every day, priests minutely examine the law and endlessly chant complicated sutras.

Before doing that, though, they should learn how to read the love letters sent by the wind and rain, the snow and moon."

*   *   *

3
Deeper Encounters

Whenever I speak to people about an interest in Yoga, a large majority automatically think I am just referring to various postures, stretches and physical exercises associated with what is an immensely rich, vibrant and multifaceted tradition. It is odd that outside most Yoga groups and organisations so little is known about other practices and teachings, especially as five principal Yoga teachers who are known in the West – Vivekananda, Yogananda, Aurobindo, Muktananda and Ramana Maharshi – are not particularly known for teachings on posture work.

One of the first yogis I took instruction from was a wonderful Tantric master called Jammu Maharaj. When I first met him, he was in his early 80s. He was slight in build but possessed a dynamic presence that would light up a room when he entered. He came to England twice a year. Before moving to bigger premises, I first met him while he was staying in a small modest apartment above an Indian Cash and Carry on the borders of East London.

Unfortunately there has been a lot of misconceptions written about Tantric yogis and their tradition. But within schools such as Kashmir Shaivism and Maharaji's Yoga the important and central teachings are about an *inclusion of life* and owning and transforming all negative parts of ourselves as a path to wholeness (a contemporary word that has connections with holiness). It was interesting to hear Cambridge biologist Rupert Sheldrake give a talk at St. James's Church, Piccadilly, a few years back. He mentioned that out of all the Indian traditions he had looked at, it was Kashmir Shaivism that shared the closest similarities with contemporary scientific understanding about creation and the universe, such as how an underlying consciousness and creativity pervade everything.

Within the Yoga traditions, particularly Tantra, the creative and unitive power of God in all things is looked upon as Shakti: the active divine Mother energy, which continuously interacts with *prakrti*/Nature and brings all things into being. It should be mentioned that neither the female nor the male forms of divinity are seen as separate from or inferior to one another in Tantric Yoga. "Within Shiva there is Shakti; within Shakti there is Shiva. I see no difference between them; they are like the moon and the moon-light", a Tantric text entitled *Siddha Siddhanta Paddhati* by Guru Goraksanatha informs us. It was through my contact with Jammu and his help that I more fully recognised the creative presence of Shakti energy whilst following his practices.

English Weather, Cricket, Apple Macs, and Integral Yoga

It was the daughter of the famous Indian singer Jagjit Singh, who not only gave me several large works by the systemiser of modern Integral Yoga, Sri Aurobindo, but in 1992 also arranged an audience for me and my friend Glyn with M. P. Pandit, who lived at the Sri Aurobindo Ashram in Pondicherry, India and was the personal secretary to the Mother (Mirra Alfassa, a spiritual collaborator of Aurobindo). Pandit was a delightful and humble man, who was known for both his informed talks and books on Aurobindo and the Mother's teachings. Our meeting turned out to be memorable for more than one reason. First, Pandit wanted to speak about the English weather. Next, he wanted to talk about cricket, though neither I nor Glyn knew much about the game. And then, because he asked what I did for a living and I mentioned graphics as one of my professions, he wanted to know my views on Apple Macs and various computer programmes! Only after that did he start to answer questions Glyn and I had, share his experiences with Aurobindo and the Mother and his vast knowledge of Integral Yoga.

Pandit was keen to point out that Integral Yoga was about engagement with life, not a retreat from it. Work, he told us, was very much a part of the ashram's daily activities. For "All life is yoga", Aurobindo famously once said. The central teachings focus on an integration of different spiritual practices and being responsibly active in the world. Though various paths are recognised as beneficial in Aurobindo's system, because of different temperaments and people's individual psychology, it is accepted that not everyone will discover the same things as helpful – apart from wholesome social engagement, which is pretty much seen as indispensable for living in accordance with a global vision. Years later I read one of Pandit's talks in which he pointed out that it was recognised within Aurobindo's teachings that not everyone could meditate in traditional Yogic ways. But this did not imply there weren't other valid practices that could be undertaken.

Overall, Aurobindo's teachings encompass numerous areas and wisdom about freedom, peace, justice, education, evolutionary science, creativity and the environment. As in Tantric traditions, worldly life is not looked upon as an illusion (in Hindu traditions the word 'maya' often means illusion, but in early teachings it meant creative power), but *real* and as an *essential facet* of spiritual life. Similar to Teilhard de Chardin, Aurobindo recognised the existence of a creative divine mind and intelligence (termed 'the Supermind' by Aurobindo) that is ever-present and continuously expressing itself in and through its workings, seeking to encourage all life and activity to a point of spiritual unity.

This, in both Aurobino and de Chardin's writings, is not a mechanistic evolution nonchalantly pushed from behind towards an aimless future (a popularly held concept that is in fact at least a hundred years out of date with contemporary scientific thinking), but about the divine drawing all things towards itself to a supreme point of mystical unity (the omega point in de Chardin's writings). As a Christian, Teilhard de Chardin saw Christ as the creative energy and loving heart of the cosmos, with the power to unite all things together and animate them into new expressions of community. Whether Aurobindo and de Chardin were completely right or not remains to be seen and is a matter of personal belief. Though when we think of and experience the creativity of life as primarily about continuous evolvement, we recognise it invariably seeking a healthy balance within a larger scheme of things.

Some of de Chardin's ideas have gone on to influence important pioneers in Earth centred movements, such as Thomas Berry. Aurobindo's grand synthesis has influenced popular writers such as Ken Wilber and the founding of the California Institute for Integral Studies, Auroville, the Sri Aurobindo Centre for International Education and, of course, the Ashram itself, which helps to support local arts and crafts cottage industries and farmers and is still an important spiritual force for many.

Yoga as Wholeness or Separation?

Questions about whether Yoga is a path of extreme ascetic detachment from the world, or one of wholeness, integration and active involvement in life is an old one. The answer lies in where the emphasis is placed, how teachings are interpreted and what practices are followed. The teachings of the Bhagavad Gita show the divine figure Krishna encouraging Arjuna to fulfil his princely duties instead of renouncing them for a path with no responsibilities (2:5).

Krishna even points out that there cannot be any true disengagement from physical life (3:5) and that through a predominant mix of Bhakti and Karma Yoga (devotional and nonattached selfless actions) along with focusing the mind/meditation and the insight of Jnana Yoga, a path could be found leading to ultimate union with him (18:65).

Selfless work, as promoted in teachings of Karma Yoga and about *svadharma* (fulfilling social obligations), can focus on healthy engagement with life. However, in Brahmanical/Orthodox Hinduism, particular roles and duties can be assigned to specific castes that keep everyone in their place in order to maintain an exclusive and archaic belief in ritual purity amongst higher caste members. In contrast to the Brahmanical tradition, numerous Yoga teachers have been more inclusive.

Within Indian daily life the sacred and the secular are not sharply divided into different camps because of panentheistic understandings of divinity interacting within and beyond all and, as the Dalai Lama informs us in his important book *Beyond Religion*, because of unantagonistic attitudes within India's secular society towards religious and spiritual beliefs. Many yoginis and yogins choose to follow a similar path to the Buddha by walking middle ground between extreme renunciation of and being fully involved in worldly affairs and often give practical instructions on how people can conduct themselves in regular life, consider practices of non-harmfulness, and be more aware of and responsible for their actions. The implications for how such teachings relate to ways we treat other species, Mother

Earth and people are obviously enormous.

In the book *The Integrity of the Yoga Darsana*, the writer Ian Whicher puts forward an excellent case for Patanjali's teachings being about the integration of numerous parts of ourselves – the ethical, physical, emotional, mental and spiritual. This approach ties in with other wisdom traditions that are life affirming and is the central message of many contemporary teachers such as Michael Stone who runs a Buddhist and Yoga *sangha* (community) in Toronto, Canada, where students are encouraged to find a skilful balance between actions that benefit the world and a healthy loosening up of attachments to material gains. It means rising above our everyday entanglements, and combining discernment with individual, emotional, social and environmental responsibility. This allows us to respect and to participate selflessly in life with understanding and to display compassionate empathy towards others. Both awareness of our actions and respect for the sacredness of life are highly prized in Yogic wisdom. This of course includes protecting and preserving life.

Christians Engaging with Indian Traditions

In Martin Ganeri's *Hinduism from a Catholic Perspective*, he treads a razor's edge in order to demonstrate much that is of value in various Hindu, Vedanta and Yogic traditions of India, though points out that he believes the non-dual philosophy of Advaita Vedanta is "clearly incompatible with the articles of Christian faith". He believes this because the absolute monism of later Advaita Vedanta excludes the notion of a personal God. Ganeri's small book draws much from the Second Vatican Council to point out important aspects of Hinduism such as the Vedanta and Yoga traditions. His writings show that even within mainstream fields of Catholicism there can be healthy, open and enriching dialogues with Hindus and practitioners of different Yogic paths, particularly those with more devotional understandings of God as a creator.

Following in the footsteps of Swami Paramarubyananda (aka Fr Jules Monchanin) and Swami Abhisihktananda (aka Fr Henri le Saux), one of the most high profile figures in recent decades to have achieved a Hindu-Christian fusion has been the English born Benedictine monk Bede Griffiths, who was also known in the final years of his life as Swami Dayananda, meaning 'bliss of compassion'. In contrast to Ganeri, both Abhisihktananda and Griffiths saw few problems in marrying Christian, Advaita Vedantic and Yogic non-dual teachings. In Bruno Barnhart's masterful comprehensive anthology of Griffiths's principle writings, *One Light*, he mentions how Griffiths thought of himself as a Christian yogi. In his anthology, Barnhart mentions how Griffiths contrasted Patajanjali's Yoga, in which the final stage of liberation is thought to promote a separation of spirit from Nature, with the Integral Yoga of Aurobindo, which embraces both an ascendance and descendence of spirit consciousness into matter. Griffiths also drew upon Teilhard de Chardin's stages of evolution and discoveries in quantum physics, microbiology and transpersonal psychology from the West. Barnhart also points out that for Griffiths, the word 'spirit' signified both the *atman* of the Hindu and Yoga traditions (the true Self and spark of divinity within that is at one with the divinity in all/*Brahman*), as well as the Holy Spirit of the Christian tradition.

Dion Foster also highlights how Griffiths's teachings are intertwined with an understanding of a cosmic whole and of the Cosmic Christ. Griffiths himself informs us that, "We need to develop the sense of the cosmic whole and of a way of relating to the world around us as a living being which sustains and nourishes us and for which we have responsibility".

Swami Amaldas, who died in 1990, was also a member of the Shantivanam Ashram in South India where Griffiths was based for the last two and half decades of his life. Amaldas also became another recognised authority on Yoga and wrote a detailed manual, *Christian Yogic Meditations*, that outlined various practices taught in the ashram. Since Griffiths's passing in 1993, his successor, John Martin Sahajananda, has continued Paramarubyananda, Abhisihktananda and Griffiths's Indian-Christian experiment at Shantivanam and their significant influence (especially Griffiths's) in both the East and West has continued to this day.

At the foot of Chamundi Hill in Mysore there is a centre that is little known outside of India, Anjali Ashram, which was founded in 1979 by the Christian priest Swami Amalorananda, who was born in a small village in Tamil Nadu and successfully married and synthesised his Christian faith with his Indian roots. Services are performed there throughout the year that incorporate both Christian, Hindu and Yogic rituals, prayers, teachings, hymns, mantras, songs and poems. On the two occasions I visited with friends, I was overwhelmed by both the joy and mystical presence of the divine in their services. Aims promoted by the ashram include building a multi-religious community, promoting Indian spirituality and working towards the promotion of justice, freedom, education and *ahimsa* (nonviolence), which Amalorananda points out in the book *Atma Purna Anubhava*, includes a, "respect for all life [that] extends beyond human persons to every form of life including vegetation and animals". I have included some photos taken at the ashram in this book because it is so unknown outside of India.

Other notable twentieth century Christian mystics who actively submerged themselves in East-West dialogues have been the American Trappist monk Thomas Merton, who sadly died too young and had up to his death focussed predominantly on Buddhist and Far Eastern teachings, and the English Benedictine monk John Main, who was introduced to Eastern meditation and mantra by the renowned Yoga master Swami Sivananda, and partly through that encounter, began to reassess some of the wisdom of the early Desert Mothers and Fathers and went on to teach numerous Christians how to use the ancient Aramaic prayer *Maranatha*, meaning 'come lord', as a form of contemplative practice. This then led to the formation and spread of the highly popular World Community for Christian Meditation movement, the work of which

Left: Meditation Hall, Anjali Ashram, Mysore, India.
Top right: Section of a main door leading to the ashram.
Bottom right (left to right): Devadasa (Glyn Edwards), Swami Gnanajyothi
(Fr. Louis, present Acharya guru of Anjali Ashram), and Santoshan
(Stephen Wollaston) at Anjali Ashram, New Year's Day 2010.

continues to this day and is now fronted by Fr. Laurence Freeman, who has written about environmental concerns in the movement's newsletter and against animal experimentation in his book *Jesus the Teacher Within*.

In a talk given at a seminar on meditation, celebrating the life and teachings of John Main, Freeman mentioned how he ran a Back to Basics course for troubled teenagers suffering from depression and low self-esteem, on which they would spend time in the countryside learning how to do without many of the things they had come to see as so important in their lives, such as fashion accessories, mobile phones and other electrical and often expensive, yet ultimately expendable, gadgets and items. He mentioned how they would often complain at first, but by the end of the course they found a different set of values that gave them a deeper and more lasting sense of happiness, as well as confidence in themselves. They found themselves becoming more contented when their lives were simplified and began to appreciate the true beauty of Nature and being able to relate authentically to others on less superficial levels.

*   *   *

4

Embracing our Earth Mother & Responding to Her Call

The essential call of spiritual work is interwoven with practical living and actions that bring benefit to others. In Edward O. Wilson's *The Creation* he points out that "each species, however inconspicuous and humble it may seem to us at this moment, is a masterpiece of biology, and well worth saving... Prudence alone dictates that we act quickly to prevent the extinction of species and with it, the pauperization of Earth's ecosystems".

Instead of raising awareness of the rape of the natural world and the mass genocide of hundreds of species, popular media have numbed many people's senses and distracted vast majorities from activist passions. "Today, the Sixth Mass Extinction is happening under our very noses! Every day, an estimated 150 species are becoming extinct. We are talking here about entire species compromising tens of thousands and even millions of individual plants, insects, and animals", respected Yoga practitioner and scholar

Georg Feuerstein wrote in his insightful co-authored book *Green Yoga*.

Gaia is obviously suffering. Feuerstein went as far to write she was *dying*. One would hope that few people would question that we humans are responsible for her current suffering and planetary climate changes. Yet I still meet people who tell me they 'can't see any signs of global warming with all the floods and extremes of bad weather we are experiencing' and how 'Earth has undergone temperature fluctuations before and the climate changes we are witnessing have nothing to do with human activity'. One person even told me how he 'didn't accept any of the statistics in Al Gore's award winning documentary *An Inconvenient Truth* because Gore earns a good wage and is flown about in an aeroplane'! Obviously the majority of people concerned about environmental issues and eco-justice aren't necessarily wealthy and logic alone should tell us that pumping toxic fumes into the atmosphere and discarding poisonous chemicals and waste into the oceans, rivers and ground is going to have negative consequences.

It seems there is still work to be done to raise awareness of what is the most urgent and important spiritual crises Earth has ever witnessed. Unfortunately, one problem has been that mainstream movements in traditions such as Christianity and Yoga have not moved quickly enough to become actively involved in issues about our planet's important ecological crises – influential prophetic voices in both traditions have often come from the minority rather than the majority. Nor have they always helped to forge a healthy bond between beliefs and caring for Mother Earth, even though many of the great mystics in numerous traditions were only too aware of their interactive relationship with the sacredness of Nature and how Nature can inspire and replenish us. God and Spirit are and have often been seen as being *someplace else* with predominantly masculine qualities – particularly in mainstream monotheistic traditions – and the focus has all too often been placed primarily on physical life as either an *illusion* and/or something to be *renounced*, and on *human* afterlife, *human* evolvement and *human* relationships that unhealthily place our species above and separate from others and the natural world.

Even when there is wide acknowledgement of environmental issues amongst students and teachers of Christianity and Yoga, there can still be little done that goes beyond church and temple buildings and the meditation cushion or exercise mat. Practices of prayer or meditation in any tradition that include prayers or visualisations for healing our planet can be greatly beneficial and help us to build a stronger awareness of the suffering of other species. But a prayerful/meditative life needs to be interwoven with actions. Authentic spiritual work is only truly effective when it walks hand-in-hand with exterior compassionate work. The central teachings are there in all the great traditions, but we often need to work hard to uncover layers of other people's agendas and interpretations to discover their true meaning and fully embody their wisdom.

In a relatively recent attempt to address beliefs some

have about God only caring about humans and to promote steps to prevent further environmental damage being done to the planet, Christians from various denominations in America compiled *God's Earth is Sacred: An Open Letter to Church and Society.* The letter primarily placed its focus on the biblical idea of stewardship as found in Genesis 2:15, which places humans as managers and carers of Nature and, therefore, puts humans in a different role to other life forms: "The Lord God took the man and put him in the garden of Eden to till it and keep it."

In addition to verse 2:15, Genesis mentions God giving humans dominion over fish, birds, cattle, wild animals and every living thing that moves and creeps on Earth and to fill the Earth and subdue it (1:26-28). Much ink has been spilt since the 1960s speculating what the words 'dominion' and 'subdue' mean in context to other passages in Genesis. Some have "wrongly claimed to have uncovered the root cause of the environmental predicament", Chris Park writes in his helpful book *Caring for Creation.* I must admit to having once believed there was a case for the claim. On a deeper reading of a well-researched chapter by Carol J. Adams in a *Faith Embracing all Creatures* and passages in Genesis themselves, it looks like Park was right to state the claim is wrong, though it could still be argued that misinterpretations of Genesis may have influenced humankind's destructive interactions with the natural world. What is *clear* is since the industrial age humans have sought to control and plunder Nature on a grand scale, which has invariably ended in disaster.

The word 'dominion' is used for the Hebrew word *radah* and 'subdue' for *kabas*. Though *radah* is used in other places in the Hebrew Bible to signify such things as power, control and authority of one individual or group over another, it seems fair to say that interpreting either *radah* or *kabas* to imply something malevolent doesn't make sense in the context of other passages in Genesis, which describe the first humans as being instructed to look after the Earth and as vegetarians without any right to inflict harm on animals and how God was pleased with all that had been created and its goodness. David Bland, who has taken an interest in holistic dimensions of the Bible writes that, "Humans are given dominion, not domination; they are caregivers, not exploiters... We do unto creation as God has done unto us; we express love and care towards the world". Similarly, in Karen Armstrong's interpretation of early sections of Genesis she mentions that, "The world was not to be exploited ... but treated with respect ... Human beings did not own the world; they could not ransack its treasures indiscriminately".

Sacredness of Earth and Nature

Philosophical and Yogic paths of the Hindu tradition are about realising the *atman* and *Brahman* relationship, realising that our true Self is interconnected with all. For Christian mystics such as Hildegard of Bingen it was the Word, the Cosmic Christ that was seen in everything, in every plant, animal and human being. Jesus often drew upon Nature for his parables. The Gospel of Thomas tells us that Jesus taught about discovering the kingdom of heaven both within and all around us. Former Archbishop William Temple noticed how, "Jesus taught men [and women] to see the operation of God in the regular and the normal – in the rising of the sun and the falling of the rain and the growth of the plant". As with all great teachings, there is a need to reflect on what they imply in order to discover their deeper meaning. Though it takes little imagination to see how Jesus's wisdom can be expanded and considered just as relevant for today's world and problems as they were for his own historical years on Earth, which many green conscious and other progressive Christians have done of course. For Gaia is calling us to come together through interspiritual, interfaith and deep ecumenical work in order to bring about healthy changes and establish both sustainable and mutually beneficial harmony with her.

For some this is seen as a looking back process, about learning from the mistakes of the past and relearning things that we have forgotten. On one side of the coin, there is great wisdom to this approach. Indigenous cultures and early spiritual traditions seem to have much to teach us about ways in which we can get back in touch and be at one with the natural world. I once heard about someone finding ancient grains of corn that were found in a two thousand year old Egyptian tomb. When the corn was planted, it miraculously grew. Although the early Egyptian culture has long-since disappeared and we now have modern methods of turning corn into edible food, the grains themselves were still living and could easily be cultivated and used with contemporary knowledge and understanding for the nourishment of people today. I mention this, as it illustrates why many people find some of the great wisdom and mystical traditions of the past to be so enriching, as the insights, teachings and practices of different ages can still be deeply beneficial and profound forces in people's ongoing spiritual growth. Such forces have helped people bring about healthy changes within their lives and within the world. For many, they are integral seeds for cultivating wholesome unity with life.

On the other side of the coin, I have a friend who is predominantly drawn to contemporary knowledge, scientific understanding and more modern spiritual perspectives, and does not see why we need to waste our time exploring teachings from other ages. He has a valid point and obviously everyone is entitled to decide for themselves from where they find their inspiration and understanding of life and spirituality. I personally find much wisdom in the Buddha's approach to such arguments and prefer walking a middle path between two extremes. I feel that we need not completely dismiss wisdom that has gone before, nor ignore what contemporary knowledge and inspiration has to reveal. For to dismiss completely the wisdom, spiritual insights and practices of any age is to overlook the creativity of the divine continuously revealing itself in different ways.

Yet I would not wish to encourage a rose-tinted glasses view of all that has gone before. Nor do I wish to claim that all religions, mystical and spiritual paths are *predominantly* green in their beliefs or that it is always easy to find prophetic Nature centred teachings within them. There are sane reasons for keeping a safe distance from anyone seeking to undermine contemporary inspiration and wisdom because of a belief in ancient scripture having all the answers. For we are living in different times and facing problems early cultures and teachers could not have imagined. The fact that humankind can wipe out much of Earth's inhabitants with nuclear weapons, or can have a devastating effect on Nature's biodiversity and ecological balance because of irresponsible farming methods, the plundering of natural resources, polluting the air and discarding harmful wastes, were not things that either Jesus or early Yoga adepts faced in their Earthly lifetimes. We do not look at the world in the same way our grandparents did when they were our age. Scientifically, culturally, sociologically, politically, psychologically and ethically we have changed and have new, fresh and many relevant perspectives about life and spirituality.

But within our growing and changes of perception we have lost important social bonds that once supported and gave us a wholesome sense of purpose, belonging and community. This is certainly true for many outside the boundaries of *healthy* religious or spiritual movements (I deliberately use the word 'healthy' here as there are communities that obviously aren't and aim to control and separate people from others and from the collective responsibilities we share for each other and all species). Many are now on their own if things do not work out. Partly because of mass urbanisation and beliefs in mass produced material goods having magical powers to bring us lasting happiness, many have lost authentic connections with Gaia and the sacred elements of life that early cultures and traditions once recognised.

We need to realise that what is fed into our unconscious minds will affect our conscious awareness and actions. It is because of past conditioning that we see ourselves as physically disconnected to exterior life and have limited our compassionate natures to only a certain few we consider as being close to us. Our conditioned senses have created the appearance of being singular and distinctly separate from other people, species, objects and phenomena around us. Yet not only do mystics of the Christian and Yogic traditions tell us that this is a wrong perception, but also quantum physicists have discovered this to be true. On a sub-atomic level there is no clear boundary between different forms of life, objects and phenomenon. Similarly the research of Rupert Sheldrake into morphogenetic fields and resonance also shows an interconnected intelligence in Nature, of which we are all integral parts. These findings do not imply that all of what we experience is an illusion in the physical world, but that we are being tricked by misperceptions and are not seeing things as they really are – as an interconnected and sacred whole.

Prophetic Wisdom

There is an urgent cry for us to wake up and re-establish kinship with both our fellow humans and the natural world, with our global sister and brother species, such as many of the endangered and magnificent creatures walking and living on the African plains and living in the world's ancient rain forests. Prophetic voices of our age such as Thomas Berry have called for recognition of a single Earth community, a single community of life. Berry emphasised 'the great work' that lies ahead. But great changes will only happen when people band together and get fully behind ideas. We only have to look at how the equal rights movement in America led to reforms in legislation. The seemingly impossible can be achieved when we have the vision and driving force of prophets such as Martin Luther King, Jr. and Mahatma Gandhi. It is a difference between falling apart into hopelessness or finding empowerment through uniting and working together.

Berry termed the new era of spirituality needed for our times 'the Ecozoic era': an era where humans live in reciprocal relationships with Earth and the Earth community. This is subtly different to stewardship, as it puts us on a more equal footing with the rest of Nature, instead of seeing humans as the peak of creation. Berry felt that we had lost our links with Earth because we no longer share myths and stories our early ancestors had that helped them find close bonds with the natural world. Yet in the light of contemporary science, most ancient stories and myths have lost their power and relevance to the age in which we now live. Our understanding of how stars, galaxies and organic life came into being no longer matches a lot of their contents (though in some Yogic teachings, everything is seen to emerge from a cosmic form of *bindu*, a source point and centre of energy, which is perhaps comparable to the Big Bang theory).

Because of this, what is now seen as a New Earth/ Universe Story (what scientist now know about the unfolding of the universe from the Big Bang to the formation and diversity of life on Earth) was recognised by Berry and the evolutionary cosmologist Brian Swimme to be needed for humankind to reconnect with its roots and the age old quest for discovering meaning and purpose, why we are here, where we are going and the unique and essential roles we and other species have in a spiritual universe. But unlike ancient creation myths – as Joel Primack and Nancy Ellen Abrams point out in their informative book *View from the Centre of the Universe* – the New Story would have to be a contemporary factual and flexible account that is not solely bound to just one tradition. It needs to be a part of an ongoing search for truth, based on new insights and discoveries which will help us to build harmonious communities where everyone feels valued, is able to use their abilities, and express their creativity in fertile and supportive environments.

On the whole, contemporary Western societies have lost something essential by no longer possessing shared beliefs and teachings and not realising that those beliefs and teachings can aid us in awakening to significant relationships with Earth. When we have nothing to bring us together or to help us find a deep sense of belonging, we often clog-up our lives with material products we do not need and immerse ourselves in pursuits that lead us away from an authentic spirituality that can profoundly enrich us.

The very first flaring forth of creation, Ellen Bernstein tells us in *The Green Bible*, was seen by early rabbis as the first revelation of God in the universe. Before any God of scripture or God of humans, there has been a God of Nature. For God has been working in and through Nature for longer than any human centred spiritual or religious tradition. Matthew Fox has popularly highlighted teachings that honour Nature and our spiritual and creative being as *original blessing*, which has strong roots in many traditions that affirm our original goodness – the blessing of life and the spiritual gifts we all possess and have the potential for. As previously referred to, the poetic first chapter of Genesis, which was possibly written as early as the tenth century BCE, informs us that, "God saw everything that [she/] he had made, and indeed, it was very good" (1:31).

If we consider how various people, cultures and communities have different beliefs and things they value, such as money, power or being compassionate to *all* beings, we see how these will influence individuals, groups and nations differently. For this reason it is crucial to look at our values and other influences in our societies and communities. Becoming more actively loving, which has associations with the heart chakra, *anahata*, in Indian traditions, is central in the universal wisdom of Jesus and different schools of Yoga. Christianity and Yoga have essential teachings about love, non-harm and suffering, how we need to respond to another's pain with compassion.

Any harm deliberately brought against another will hurt

us in return because we ourselves have brought selfishness and violence instead of benevolent qualities into the world of which we are a part. The Apostle Paul wrote about awareness of 'the mind of Christ' (1 Corinthians 2:16 and Philippians 2:5), which is about awakening to the same inclusive, loving and caring consciousness as Jesus, and wrote about gaining and being 'nothing' if we do not have love (1 Corinthians 13:2-3). Jesus's teachings invariably focus on a life centred in the immanent presence of the divine and freedom from impractical rules and customs that restrict displays of forgiveness, generosity, hospitality, kindness and peace-making actions.

The founder of the Institute for Spiritual Awareness and former Catholic monk Jim Marion looks at Paul's saying in Philippians ("Let the same mind be in you that was in Christ Jesus") in the book *Putting on the Mind of Christ*. He draws heavily on Ken Wilber's stages of development and makes masterful links between Paul's saying and Jesus's mention of the Kingdom of Heaven, which Marion sees as a metaphor for a transformed, integral and inclusive state of consciousness and new way of looking at the world.

If we embrace the whole – including Earthly life, the more than human life, and transformative and compassionate actions – in order to untangle ourselves from unhealthy patterns of desiring things we do not need, or from rejecting wholesome ways of living because they force us to reassess how we view the rights of other people and species, we will arrive at a more centred, nourishing and spiritual place. In the midst of such awakenings we tap into the power of authentic being and instead of obscuring who we truly are, face and work through denied levels and difficult stages and find ways of opening to purer qualities of heart that embrace the welfare of others. Allowing all things and existence to enter into and touch our individual lives deeply, inspires us into wholesome activities and actions, such as giving our time and help freely and unconditionally when external life calls for our assistance.

Healthy Christian and Yogic practices are about being awake to this potential, and the abilities and possibilities that are available to us in every moment, which can lead us to being spontaneously creative and to participate skilfully in life as it unfolds. For within everyone there is the creative divine impulse, and when we create, we take part in and celebrate the creativity that exists within the universe – we become co-creators. This active form of spirituality is intrinsically bound-up with wholeness and compassion. We should not confuse it with egotistical ideas or psychologically unhealthy states of creativity, but realise that it is bound-up with that which can naturally flow from us as a result of wholesome connections with all. It plugs us in to the dance of divine creation – though that connection has always been there, we may not have been aware of it until now – in the quest for cosmic harmony and balance. Through this we are led to a deeper sense of what is truly sacred.

However, we cannot force ourselves to awaken to this understanding and active path of spiritual engagement. For it needs to arise naturally within our hearts as a response to our interconnectedness with all and sharing in others' pains and joys. The spiritual roots of this are found not only in the Christian mystical traditions, but also in Tantra Yoga, connected with various chakras and with Shakti (the creative divine Mother energy), and with aspects of Sufi, Buddhist, Daoist, ancient Celtic, African Bush people's, Australian Aboriginal, Native American, Hasidic Jewish and Neo-Pagan spirituality. It is as old as creation itself because of its connections with the creative force and mind that has pervaded the universe since its birth.

*   *   *

5

Mending the Broken Pieces

D rawing on a saying by the Church of Scotland minister and founder of the Iona Community, George MacLeod, poet, teacher and former warden of Iona Abbey, John Philip Newell, writes in his insightful book *Christ of the Celts* that "in the Celtic tradition, Christ comes to show us that matter matters. Creation will be saved only if we learn to revere matter... Christ leads us not away from matter but more deeply into the stuff of the universe and the stuff of daily life and relationship".

Many early Celtic Christians drew heavily on the Gospel of John for their inspiration and identified with the disciple Jesus loved, who is described in John as laying close to Jesus's chest (13:25) and therefore could have heard and possibly felt Jesus's own beating heart. The strongly creation centred spirituality of the early Celtic Christians often sought to re-enact this passage of the Bible by seeking to find God's physical presence in the natural world and the wonders of Nature. Their art, prayers, teachings, poems and writings are full of deep mystical insights into the activities of Nature.

For the 14th and 15th century English mystic Julian of Norwich, God was seen in everything – the human body and the body of creation – and she insisted, as the early Celtic tradition had done, that both Nature and grace were one. Francis of Assisi praised God in all creatures, in brother sun, sister moon, the stars, wind, air, clouds and all weathers, through which God gave sustenance.

More recently, the Brazilian theologian Leonardo Boff, who has worked for the liberation of the poor in Brazil for several decades, has combined Christian liberation theology with environmental concerns since the 1990s, declared that rights should not be limited to just humans nor to nations, since "all things in nature are citizens, have rights, and deserve respect and reverence … Today, the common good is not exclusively human; it is the common good of all nature". In an outline of the first of three principle beliefs of the Greek Orthodox Church, John Chryssavgis, who is an advisor to the Ecumenical Patriarch on ecological issues in America, pointed out that no part of the natural world could be divorced from environmental concerns and the loving care of God.

Thomas Berry's Earth centred teachings show him seeking to encourage Christians to address environmental issues, even at the expense of putting the Bible on the shelf for 30 years. An idea that in fact created some criticism of his teachings. Instead of seeing the universe as a collection of separate objects to be exploited, he promoted an understanding of all life and things as an interactive communion of divine subjects. In place of anthropocentric/ human centred teachings, Berry emphasised experience of psychic and spiritual dimensions of the universe and Earth-life that recognised important links between wholeness and holiness and the sacredness of all. He particularly noticed how over emphasised beliefs about human transcendence and human spirituality had alienated people from the natural world and sometimes drew upon the role of shamans in his books to highlight how we had lost crucial connections with Nature that shamanic cultures recognised.

For many Hindu yoginis and yogins, God and *prakrti* (Nature) are one and the same. Though on a lower level of understanding, *prakrti* is also seen as responsible for causing the appearance of separateness, misperceptions and blindness of our interconnectedness with all things. The Srimad Bhagavata Purana (11.2.41) states that, "Ether, air, fire, water, earth, planets, all creatures, directions, trees and plants, rivers and seas, they all are organs of God's body; remembering this, a devotee respects all species". It is through both reverence and a respect for what is seen as a divinity in all things and all things in the divine that students of Yoga are expected to maintain harmonious relationships.

Waking Up

When we penetrate the deeper dimensions of Christianity and Yoga, we discover elements of Nature mysticism submerged within them – we find holy wells and mountains, sacred trees and rivers, and elemental forces of earth, air, fire and water woven into the tapestry of their practices and insights. The ancient forests of India, Ranchor Prime tells us in his book *Vedic Ecology*, also share direct links to India's spiritual past, as many of India's great teachers would have lived and imparted their wisdom within them. Yoga traditions see the universe composed of *prana* (creative primordial energy), which links with *akasa* (primordial Nature and/or ether), from which material forms and elements are produced. Tantric teachings view *prana* as a lower manifestation or instrument of Shakti and her interactions with Nature.

In Matthew Fox and Rupert Sheldrake's *Natural Grace*, they mention how such understandings of the universe and the sacred appear to be embedded within the human psyche and how there seems to be an essential need for us to relate to the natural world in unique ways such as pilgrimages to holy places – which interestingly have their own special energies that go beyond set beliefs and attract people from all faiths as well as none – or rituals that expand our awareness of the sacredness of life.

In fact, any experience of deep contact with Nature often helps in the healing process in times of stress and suffering, and leads us to discover wider and more holistic perspectives of existence that inevitably enrich us in profound and life enhancing ways. Doctors now recognise that simply walking in Nature is one of the best exercises for physical health and mental well-being. As a Londoner I often feel the need to be quiet and spend time in places of great beauty such as Kew Gardens and Epping Forest, which are on the outskirts of London, when the pressures of life make my heart feel heavy. Deep within the majority of children and adults there is a natural sense of awe and wonder experienced when they look up at the multitude of stars that can be seen at night or contemplate the rich beauty of Earth and its colossal array of plants, flowers, trees, insects, animals and birds.

At weekends and on holidays our love of Nature often impels us to escape our brick and concrete buildings to find time to rediscover this natural element of spirituality – to be rejuvenated and spontaneously healed whilst being amongst the dazzling colours and aromatic smells of diverse plants and the amazing wildlife of the countryside, or by contemplating breath-taking rolling hills, majestic mountain ranges, dappled textures of sunlight penetrating lush forests, or the crashing and rolling waves of a roaring sea. Music and song, which is important in many people's lives and has the power to heal and unite people, is an awesome product of Nature. For many of Earth's magnificent creatures of the sky, land, oceans and rivers have been singing to and musically improvising with each other for millions of years – long before us humans arrived in the evolutionary history of this magnificent evolving and living planet.

Yet because of mass urbanisation and consumerist pressures and through seeing the world full of resources to plunder and exploit we often don't realise that much of what we enjoy about the natural world will not be around for long if we don't make dramatic U-turns in our lifestyles and values. Interestingly, all spiritual and mystical traditions are about waking up, becoming more aware of life, seeing how all things are interrelated, how skilful and unskilful actions have consequences (karma in Indian traditions), and through this understanding to become more responsible for our impact on Earth-life. Both Christian and Yogic spirituality teach about embracing our humanity, working with and transforming our destructive tendencies in order to uncover profound wisdom that spills into the actions of our daily lives. However, it needs to be clear that these deeper dimensions are not about imposing archaic moral judgements on others, but are universal truths (*sanatana*, the eternal dharma in Hinduism) about who we really are, our authentic nature, our original goodness, and how this leads to becoming naturally and spontaneously active forces for good in the world. This includes being an *activist*, which is what being a prophet is about, in whatever spiritual and compassionate way we can.

When we awaken to such profound truths and selfless ways of being and becoming, we discover a unity and wholeness that is the ground of all activity and existence. Once realised we openly embrace the workings of Nature and recognise that the tiniest of creatures or the smallest of plants can open us to deeper mysteries. Such openings are interconnected cores of spiritual and mystical insight that can lead us to more responsible living. All of the world's great spiritual traditions remind us of this and often highlight that it is not enough to just experience expanded states of awareness, but that we also need to embody and live their implications. For if *all* is a part of us and we are a part of the *all*, it then follows that every creature and species is a member of our universal family. And just as we feel a sense of connection to and naturally care about the welfare of our closest blood family members, there is a need to be in touch with realms of our being that include and care for our global sisters and brothers. It is the realisation of this reality that beckons and requires us to translate it into wholesome action.

In the Foreword to *Yoga and the Sacred Fire*, the Hindu author of several books on Ayurveda and Yoga spirituality, David Frawley, mentions how, "We are failing to adapt to our world. Instead we are trying to compel the world to accommodate us, as if we were the only species on the planet". The sacredness of life has always been there within the Hindu Yogic traditions. Being responsible for how we interact with and consider everything that surrounds us is particularly propagated in Patanjali's teachings on the *yamas* (external ethical virtues) and *niyamas* (the cultivation of inner virtues), which are the first of two important steps in the classic eight limbs of Yoga. The *yamas* and *niyamas* include non-harmfulness, truthfulness and mindful introspection. As a whole, the *yamas* and *niyamas* are looked upon as indispensable within numerous paths and schools of Yoga, though the idea of becoming a *brahmacharya* (celibate), which is also mentioned, is not considered as a strict rule by many teachers and students, as sex is not dismissed as something unsacred in the Hindu and Yoga traditions.

Interspirituality*

There are crucial threads woven through all spiritual traditions and much common ground between them, but it is never as simple as a 'one cap fits all' scenario. Because traditions change, organically evolve and take on new and different perspectives – due to issues of power, control, or beliefs in what is valid and seen as right, just and compassionate, or a bursting forth of new revelation and experience – it often leaves us with no *single* perspective that can be used to summarise the whole of any one tradition.

Discovering important ground where we can healthily come together with people from different beliefs often requires time, study, flashes of insight, wise discernment and deep reflections. It will involve being open and making mature adjustments to some of our previously held beliefs. Such steps are essential to authentic and wholesome growth. If we take a leaf from the pages of Nature, which are about diversity and equilibrium, we can learn how to go forward. If we follow her example and are maturely sensitive enough to the differences that make up our human race, and appreciate how human life is enriched by its different people, beliefs and cultures, we can start to find ways of living peacefully with one another and working together for the betterment of all.

*A term first coined by the lay-monk Wayne Teasdale.

It is no longer a case of thinking in terms of whether religious and spiritual communities should be getting involved in becoming architects of a new spirituality or not, but about realising that humankind will not be effective enough in bringing about the necessary ecological changes that are called for if they don't. This is not just about individual beliefs and what things we can do as individuals. It is also about addressing wider problems of materialism, sustainability, global responsibility, power, greed, exploitation and consumer addictions to harmful patterns of behaviour and increasingly wanting more stuff. Corporate businesses are of course only too happy for us to focus our passions on buying the latest gadgets and new items of clothing instead of concerning ourselves with environmental issues. "Collectively our global consumption of resources is 1.23 times that of our ecological footprint. That is, we humans are already using one and a quarter planet Earths. At the same time, the affluent 20 percent of the world's population controls and uses approximately 80 percent of the Earth's resources", retired Uniting Church minister Noel Preston importantly brings to our attention in the recent book *Why Weren't We Told?*

If we are to continue living with Mother Earth, we need to not only care about the diversity of life she has sought to celebrate but also learn how to read her signs, understand her ways and adapt creatively to living in harmony with her. For she does not have inexhaustible supplies. "The maternal sea is polluted, the heavens are rent, the forests are being destroyed and the deserts are increasing", Patriarch Ignatuis IV of Antioch informs us. Continuously taking what is not ours to take can only lead to a spiritual poverty of the natural world. Nonetheless, Ellen Bernstein encouragingly points out in *The Splendor of Creation* that "just as we have the power to spoil the creation, we also have the power to make it whole. We have the power to mend the earth and to mend ourselves, to sew the pieces back together again".

I fully believe that the majority of people mentioned in this book would unanimously agree that our current times need us to work together, to search passionately for a unitive spirituality that crosses all boundaries and looks for a multiple of ways to implement it for every species' and region's benefit, including Gaia's river, forest, plant, sky, mountain, grassland and ocean queendoms and kingdoms.

By embracing such an essential idea at this point in Earth's history, we might be surprised as to what we can truly achieve; it depends on both you and me and the number of wise choices we make from this point on.

Blessed are the man and the woman
who have grown beyond their greed
and have put an end to their hatred
and no longer nourish illusions.
– Psalm 1
(translated by Stephen Mitchell)

*   *   *

Bibliography

Adams, Carol J., *What About Dominion in Genesis?* Chapter in *A Faith Embracing All Creatures: Addressing Commonly Asked Questions About Christian Care for Animals – The Peaceable Series 2* (edited by Tipp York and Andy Alexis-Baker), Cascade Books, Eugene, Oregon, 2012.

Amalorananda, Swami, *Atma Purna Anubhava*, Anjali Ashram, Mysore, 2000.

Armstrong, Karen, *In the Beginning: A New Interpretation of Genesis*, Vintage Books, London, 2011 (ebook edition).

Aurobindo, Sri, *A Conception of Supermind in the Veda.* Article in *All India Magazine*, Aurobindo Society, Pondicherry, February 2004.

— , *A Greater Psychology: An Introduction to the Psychological Thought of Sri Aurobindo* (edited by A. S. Dalal), Tarcher/Putnam, New York, 2001.

— , *The Life Divine*, Sri Aurobindo Ashram, Pondicherry, 1986 (reduced facsimile edition).

Bernstein, Ellen, *Creation Theology: A Jewish Perspective.* In *The Green Bible: New Revised Standard Version* (with a foreword by Desmond Tutu), HarperOne, New York, 2008.

— , *The Splendor of Creation: A Biblical Ecology*, Cleveland, Pilgrim Press, 2005.

Berry, Thomas, *The Dream of the Earth*, Sierra Book Club, San Francisco, 1990.

— , *Evening Thoughts: Reflecting on Earth as Sacred Community* (edited by Mary Evelyn Tucker), Sierra Book Club, San Francisco, 2006.

— , *The Great Work: Our Way into the Future*, Bell Tower, New York, 1999.

— , with Clark, Thomas, *Befriending the Earth: A Theology of Reconciliation Between Humans and the Earth*, Twenty-third Publications, Mystic, Connecticut, 1991.

Berry, Thomas, and Swimme, Brian, *The Universe Story: From the First Primordial Flaring Forth to the Ecozoic Era – A Celebration of the Universe*, HarperCollins, New York, 1992.

Bland, David, quoted in *What About Dominion in Genesis?* by Carol J. Adams. In *A Faith Embracing All Creatures: Addressing Commonly Asked Questions About Christian Care for Animals – The Peaceable Series 2* (edited by Tipp York and Andy Alexis-Baker), Cascade Books, Eugene, Oregon, 2012.

Bourgeault, Cynthia, *The Wisdom Jesus: Transforming Heart and Mind*, Shambhala, Boston, Massachusetts, 2008.

Carmichael, Cassandra (managing editor), *God's Earth is Sacred: Essays on Eco-Justice*, National Council of Churches USA, Washington, 2011.

Dasgupta, Surendranath, *A History of Indian Philosophy – Volume 1*, Motilal Banarsidass, Delhi, 1992 (reprint).

Dickens, Charles, *A Tale of Two Cities* (with an introduction and note by Peter Merchant), Wordsworth Classics, 2011 (ebook edition).

Dwivedi, O. P., *Hindu Religion and Environmental Well-being*. In *The Oxford Handbook of Religion and Ecology* (edited by Roger S. Gottlieb), Oxford University Press, New York, 2006.

Easwaran, Eknath (introduced and translation by), *Bhagavad Gita*, Blue Mountain Centre of Meditation, Tomales, 2007 (ebook edition).

Ehrman, Bart D., *Lost Christianities: The Battle for Scripture and the Faiths we Never Knew*, Oxford University Press, New York, 2003.

Eliade, Mircea, *Yoga: Immortality and Freedom*, Princeton University Press, New Jersey, 1990 (reprint).

Fadiman, James, and Frager, Robert, *Personality and Personal Growth*, Harper Collins, New York, 1994 (3rd edition).

Feuerstein, Georg, *Encyclopedia Dictionary of Yoga*, Unwin, London 1990.

— , (translated by), *The Yoga-Sutras of Patanjali*, Inner Traditions International, Vermont, 1989 (reprint).

— , and Feuerstein, Brenda, *Green Yoga*, Traditional Yoga Studies, California, 2007.

Foster, Deon A., *Christ at the Centre: Discovering the Cosmic Christ in the Spirituality of Bede Griffiths*, MMA Publishers, Silverton, 2007 (ebook edition).

Fox, Matthew, *Creativity: Where the Divine and the Human Meet*, Tarcher/Putnam, New York, 2002.

— , *Hildegard of Bingen: A Saint for our Times*, Namaste Publishing, Vancouver, British Columbia, 2012.

— , *Original Blessing: A Primer in Creation Spirituality*, Tarcher/Putnam, New York, 2000 (reprint).

— , *Wrestling with the Prophets: Essays on Creation Spirituality and Everyday Life*, Tarcher/Putnam, New York, 1995.

— , and Sheldrake, Rupert, *Natural Grace: Dialogues on Creation, Darkness, and the Soul in Spirituality and Science*, Doubleday, New York, 1996.

Frawley, David, *Yoga and the Sacred Fire: Self-Realization and Planetary Transformation*, Motilal Barnarsidass, Delhi, 2001.

Freeman, Lawrence, *Jesus the Teacher Within* (with a foreword by the Dalai Lama), Canterbury Press, London, 2010.

Ganeri, Martin, *Hinduism: From a Catholic Perspective*, Catholic Truth Society, London, 2010.

Gottlieb, Roger S., *Religion and Ecology – What is the Connection and Why Does it Matter?*. In *The Oxford Handbook of Religion and Ecology* (edited by Roger S. Gottlieb), Oxford University Press, New York, 2006.

Griffiths, Bede, quotation from *Christ at the Centre: Discovering the Cosmic Christ in the Spirituality of Bede Griffiths* by Deon Foster, MMA Publishers, Silverton, 2007 (ebook edition).

— , *The One Light: Bede Griffiths' Principal Writings* (edited with a commentary by Bruno Barnhart), Templegate, Springfield, Illinois, 2001.

Ignatuis IV of Antioch, Patriarch, quotation from *A Theology of Creation in Teachings on Creation through the Ages* (edited by J. Matthew Sleeth). In *The Green Bible: New Revised Standard Version* (with a foreword by Desmond Tutu), HarperOne, New York, 2008.

Ikkyu, quotation from *Spiritual Ecology: The Cry of the Earth* (edited by Llewellyn Vaughan-Lee), Golden Sufi Centre, California, 2013.

Lama, H. H., Dalai, *Beyond Religion: Ethics for a Whole World*, Rider, London, 2011.

Main, John, *Essential Writings* (selected with an introduction by Laurence Freeman), Orbis, New York, 2002.

Marion, Jim, *Putting on the Mind of Christ: The Inner Work of Christian Spirituality* (with a foreword by Ken Wilber), Hampton Roads Publishing, Charlottesville, 2011 (ebook edition).

Meyer, Marvin (translated with an introduction by), *The Gospel of Thomas: The Hidden Sayings of Jesus* (with an interpretation by Harold Bloom), HarperSanFrancisco, New York, 1992.

Newell, J. Philip, *Christ of the Celts: The Healing of Creation*, Jossey-Bass, San Francisco, 2008.

— , *Listening for the Heartbeat of God: A Celtic Spirituality*, Society for Promoting Christian Knowledge, London, 1997.

Norwich, Julian of, *Revelations of Divine Love*, (Elizabeth Spearing translation), Penguin, London, 1998 (new edition).

Park, Chris, *Caring for Creation: Towards a Christian Environmental Theology*, self-published ebook (printed edition published by HarperCollins), 2013.

Plotkin, Bill, *Inscendence – The Key to the Great Work of Our Time: A Soulcentric View of Thomas Berry's Work*. Chapter in *Thomas Berry, Dreamer of the Earth: The Spiritual Ecology of the Father of Environmentalism – A Worldshift Book* (edited by Ervin Laszlo and Allan Combs), Inner Traditions, Rochester Vermont, 2011 (ebook edition).

Preston, Noel, *Exploring Eco-Theology*. Article in *Why Weren't We Told? A Handbook on 'Progressive' Christianity* (compiled and edited by Rex A. E. Hunt and John W. H. Smith), Polebridge Press, Salem, Oregon, 2013 (ebook edition).

Primack, Joel, and Abrams, Nancy Ellen, *The View from the Centre of the Universe: Discovering our Extraordinary Place in the Cosmos*, Fourth Estate, London, 2006.

Prime, Ranchor, *Vedic Ecology: Practical Wisdom for Surviving the 21st Century* (includes interviews with Vandana Shiva), Mandala Publishing, Novato CA, 2002.

Radhakrishnan, S., *Indian Philosophy – Volume 2*, Oxford University Press, Oxford, 1991 (4th reprint).

Rowe, Keith, *Christology (in an Evolutionary World)*. Article in *Why Weren't We Told? A Handbook on 'Progressive' Christianity* (compiled and edited by Rex A. E. Hunt and John W. H. Smith), Polebridge Press, Salem, Oregon, 2013 (ebook edition).

Santoshan (Wollaston, Stephen). Chapters from *The House of Wisdom:*

Yoga Spirituality of the East and West, by Swami Dharmananda and Santoshan, Mantra Books, Winchester and New York, 2007.

— , *Spirituality Unveiled: Awakening to Creative Life*, Earth Books, 2011.

— , *Walking a Razor's Edge*. Article in *GreenSpirit Magazine – Volume 15:1*, Spring 2013.

— , *Yogas of Action*. Article in *GreenSpirit Magazine – Volume 13:1*, Spring 2011.

Satchidananda, Sri Swami (translation and commentary by), *The Living Gita: The Complete Bhagavad Gita – A Coemmentary for Modern Readers*, Integral Yoga Publications, Buckingham, Virginia, 1988.

Stone, Michael, *Yoga for a World out of Balance: Teachings on Ethics and Social Action*, Shambhala, Boston, Massachusetts, 2009.

Taylor, Bron (edited by), *Encyclopedia of Religion and Nature – Volumes 1 and 2*, Continuum, London, 2008 (reprint).

Teilhard de Chardin, Pierre, *The Human Phenomenon* (translated by Sara Appleton-Weber), Sussex Academy Press, Brighton and Portland, 2003.

— , *Pierre Teilhard de Chardin* (writings selected with an introduction by Ursula King), Orbis Books, New York, 1999.

Temple, William, quotation from *The New Daily Study Bible: The Gospel of Mark*, by William Barclay (with an introduction by John Drane), Westminster John Knox Press, Louisville, Kentucky, 2001 (revised and updated edition).

Whicher, Ian, *The Integrity of the Yoga Darsana: A Reconsideration of Classical Yoga*, State University of New York Press, New York, 1998.

Wilson, Edward O., *The Creation: An Appeal to Save Life on Earth*, W.W. Norton and Company, New York and London, 2006.

Yogananda, Paramahansa, *Second Coming of Christ: The Resurrection of the Christ within You – Volumes 1 and 2*, Self-Realization Fellowship, Los Angeles, 2005.

DVD Reference

Freeman, Fr. Laurence (talk by), *John Main: A Celebration of his Life and Teaching*, Conference at Swanwick, UK, 2007.

Website References (January 2014)

Bhaktivedanta Manor Cow Protection Programme:
www.bhaktivedantamanor.co.uk/home/?page_id=26

Chryssavgis, John, *Christian Orthodoxy*:
www.clas.ufl.edu/users/bron/pdf

Hiebert, Theodore, *Rethinking Dominion Theology*:
www.directionjournal.org/issues/gen/art_922_.html

Mitchell, Stephen, translation for *Psalm 1*:
www.soulofthegarden.com/poem3.html

Paul II, Pope John, *Peace with God the Creator, Peace with all of Creation*:
www.conservation.catholic.org/ecologicalcrisis.htm

Quotation from Siddha Siddhanta Paddhati in an introduction to Shri Jnaneshwar's philosophy (unaccredited author), *Human Freedom and the Determination by the Will of God*:
www.yoga.econverge.in/d-_introduction.docx

Wikipedia, *Original Sin* (unaccredited author/s):
www.en.wikipedia.org/wiki/original_sin

Wikipedia, *Eastern Orthodox Church* (unaccredited author/s):
www.en.wikipedia.org/wiki/eastern_orthodox_christian_theology

Additional References

Holy Bible: New Revised Standard Version, HarperCollins e-books, San Francisco, 1989.

Renewing the Earth: An Invitation to Reflection and Action on Environment in Light of Catholic Social Teaching, United States Conference of Catholic Bishops (statement of), 2012 (ebook edition).

*   *   *

About the Author

Stephen lives in East London. He was given the name Santoshan (contentment) by an English swami in the mid-90s. In his early 20s, he played in one of London's first punk rock bands, The Wasps. He has studied transpersonal psychology, and typographic design, and holds a degree in religious studies and a post-graduate certificate in religious education from King's College London. He has served as a Council member of GreenSpirit and is a member of its editorial and publications team. In 2020 he was ordained as a OneSpirit Interfaith Foundation minister.

His books include *The House of Wisdom: Yoga Spirituality of the East and West* (coauthored, Mantra Books, 2007), *Spirituality Unveiled: Awakening to Creative Life* (Earth Books, 2011), and the multi-authored *Pathways of Green Wisdom: Discovering Earth Centred Teachings in Spiritual and Religious Traditions* (compiled and edited by Stephen for GreenSpirit in 2015).

*　　*　　*

GreenSpirit
Book Series & Other
Resources

We hope you have enjoyed reading this book, and that it has whetted your appetite to read more in this series and discover the many and varied ways in which green spirituality can be expressed in every single aspect of our lives and culture.

You may also wish to visit our website, which has a resources section, members area, information about GreenSpirit's annual events, book reviews and much more: **www.greenspirit.org.uk**

Other titles in the GreenSpirit Book Series

What is Green Spirituality? Edited by Marian Van Eyk McCain

All Our Relations: GreenSpirit Connections with the More-than-Human World. Edited by Marian Van Eyk McCain

The Universe Story in Science and Myth. By Greg Morter and Niamh Brennan

Pathways of Green Wisdom: Discovering Earth Centred Teachings in Spiritual and Religious Traditions. Edited by Santoshan (Stephen Wollaston)

Deep Green Living. Edited by Marian Van Eyk McCain

The Rising Water Project: Real Stories of Flooding, Real Stories of Downshifting. Compiled by Ian Mowll

Dark Nights of the Green Soul: From Darkness to New Horizons. Edited by Ian Mowll and Santoshan (Stephen Wollaston)

Awakening to Earth-Centred Consciousness: Selection from GreenSpirit magazine. Edited by Ian Mowll and Santoshan (Stephen Wollaston)

GreenSpirit Reflections. Compiled by Santoshan (Stephen Wollaston)

Anthology of Poems for GreenSpirits. Compiled by Joan Angus

The Lilypad List: Seven Stpes to the Simple Life. By Marian Van Eyk McCain

Meditations with Thomas Berry: With additional material by Brian Swimme. Selected by June Raymond

Free for members ebook editions

GreenSpirit
magazine

GreenSpirit magazine is free for members and is published in both print and electronic form. Each issue includes essential topics connected with Earth-based spirituality. It honours Nature as a great teacher, celebrates the creativity and interrelatedness of all life and of the cosmos, affirms biodiversity and human differences, and honours the prophetic voice of artists.

Find out more at www.greenspirit.org.uk

"For many of us, it's the spirit running through that limitless span of green organisations and ideas that anchors all the work we do. And 'GreenSpirit' is an invaluable source of insight, information and inspiration."
~ Jonathon Porritt

GreenSpirit
Path to a New Consciousness
Edited by Marian Van Eyk McCain

Only by understanding the Universe as a vast, holistic system and Earth as a unit within it can we help restore balance to that unit.

Only by placing Earth and its ecosystems – about which we now understand so much – at the centre of all our thinking can we avert ecological disaster.

Only by bringing our thinking back into balance with feeling, intuition and awareness and by grounding ourselves in a sense of the sacred in all things can we achieve a new level of consciousness.

Green spirituality is the key to a new, twenty-first century consciousness. And here is the most comprehensive book ever written on green spirituality.

Published by Earth Books
ISBN 978-1-84694-290-7

'*GreenSpirit: Path to a New Consciousness* offers numerous healing and inspiring insights; notably, that Earth and the universe are primary divine Revelation, a truth to be transmitted to our children as early and effectively as possible.'
~ THOMAS BERRY (January 2009)

Printed in Great Britain
by Amazon